OLD AFFAIRS

POEMS BY JAY MATSON

OLD AFFAIRS

OLD AFFAIRS
Poems by Jay Matson

Copyright © 2022 Jay Matson

All rights reserved. No part of this book may be reproduced or transmitted in any form or by any means, electronic or mechanical, including photocopying, recording or by any information storage and retrieval system, without written permission.
Contact: OLDAFFAIRSPOEMS@gmail.com

Design and layout | Emily de Rham

ISBN: 9798368185651

Also by Jay Matson:
CARVED ON TREES
AS I RECALL

for
Mary Margaret Jacobson

About the author:
Jay was born in Dixon, Illinois; lived most of his life in Galesburg, Illinois; also lived on a farm near Berwick, Illinois; and spent time going to school or working in St. Louis, Mexico City, Chicago, New York City, Baltimore, and San Francisco. He now resides in Berkeley, California. He was inspired to write poetry by a beloved professor, Samuel Moon, at Knox College in Galesburg.

TABLE OF CONTENTS

ADRIFT	13
AFTER RECEIVING MY FOURTH COVID SHOT I WALK HOME IN PERFECT WEATHER	14
AQUAPHOBIA	15
AS IF YOU WERE	16
AS THEY SAY	18
BALTIMORE	19
BELOVED	20
BODY & SOUL	22
CABINETMAKING	23
CANTALOUPE	25
CIGAR ROLLERS	27
CLEAR AIR	28
COLORADO	29
COMRADE	30
CUB SCOUTS	32
DEATH OF A LOVED ONE	33
DESCRIPTION OF A PHOTO DATED JUNE 1968	34
DISCHARGE OF A BASIC AIRMAN	35
DISTANCE	36
DRIVING THROUGH YELLOWSTONE	37
EDWARD AND ME	39
ELEVEN DISPLACED STANZAS	40
FISHING IN CANADA	42
FOOTBALL COACH	45
FOR AN ANONYMOUS ANCIENT FRIEND	46
HAIKU AFTER ELEVEN WEEKS OF KETO	48
HERE	49
HEY YOU	51
HIGH SCHOOL HOMECOMING DANCE	52
HOSPITAL BED	53

HOW TO WRITE A LOVE POEM	54
I KNOW, I KNOW	55
I MUST TELL YOU ABOUT MY DREAM	56
IMPRESSIONS FROM LYDIA KRÜGER'S DOSSIER	57
IMPROBABILITY	58
JOHNNY McGUIRE	59
JOHNNY UNDERHILL	60
JOURNEY OF HUMANITY	62
JUST LIKE THAT	64
LEAVING A MOTOR COURT IN UTAH	65
LOOSE THREADS AND POCKETS WITH HOLES	66
MAYBE IT WAS JUST A DREAM	67
MY GARDEN	68
MY MOTHER SURVIVED THE 1918 PANDEMIC	69
NEW YEAR'S EVE 1949	70
NOTHING HELPS	71
NOW	72
OLD FOLKS HOME	73
ON BECOMING WALLPAPER	74
ONE DAY	75
ONE SUMMER ON THE RIVER IN A BOAT NAMED MY BELLE	76
OTHERWISE	77
PARABLE OF THE SILK HANDKERCHIEF	78
PATAGONIA, AZ	79
PD	81
PLEASE HOLD	82
PORTFOLIO ROMANCE	83
REACHING YOU	84
RETURNING TO THE OCEAN AT EL GRANADA	85
ROOTS OF MY PRIVILEGE	86
SCALING DOWN	87
SEA OF HURRAHS	89
SEA RANCH	90

SEPARATE WAYS	91
SHOES IN THE ATTIC	92
SMOKING	93
SOMETIMES I FEEL LOST	94
STOP EATING HAIKU	95
SUBJECT MATTER	96
TAILLIGHTS	97
THE DISAPPEARANCE	98
THE STUDY OF PHILOSOPHY	99
THINKING OF TRAINS AT THREE IN THE MORNING	100
TOXIC MASCULINITY	101
TUSCARORA TUMBLEWEED	102
VICE PRESIDENT OF FISH	104
WE THOUGHT WE KNEW YOU	105
WHEN I DREAMED OF YOUR PAST	106
WHEN THINGS GOT INTERESTING	107
YOU CAN SEE WHERE THIS IS GOING	108
YOU KNOW THE FEELING	110

ADRIFT

Damn you, whatever force you are.
You have tricked me into thinking
I have something to say.
If I had been a lumberjack,
I'd have that reality to recall,
how I waltzed over slippery logs
in my boots with spikes,
all the way to the mill, floating
on the current, holding a long pole
freeing logjams with a tool called
a cant hook or peavy. If that was me
I would have been called a river pig
and that was a solid job title.
But I was adrift in shoe stores.
Now I am adrift in words.
I am nothing like a river pig.
Oh, to be a river pig,
waltzing over slippery logs.
I could tell you all about it.

AFTER RECEIVING MY FOURTH COVID SHOT
(2 vaccinations plus 2 boosters)
I WALK HOME IN PERFECT WEATHER

I was almost home
when a squirrel dashed out
from behind the Melaleuca tree
right by my feet. It happened fast
and might have been startling, but
it's not often I'm startled now,
probably because I'm old
and have become conditioned.
As a kid growing up after the war
(and by that I mean WWII),
back when the first trepidations
set in with *Polio!*—the word itself
was terror. To be followed
by the dreaded blacklight search
for *Ringworm!* And soon enough
the grade school nuns led us
to *Confession!* They introduced
the guilt of crossing from venial
to *Mortal Sin!* Not to mention
the *Legion of Decency!* It was
just a warm-up for facing
*The Atom Bomb! The Iron Curtain!
Red China!* In grade school,
imagine crouching under your desk
waiting for the ceiling to collapse.
You know, it conditions you
to remain somewhat unstartled
when things come along,
like *Monkeypox!*

AQUAPHOBIA

It is a condition spawned
by a crazed father
on your first vacation
when he drove non-stop
to North Dakota to visit
graves of unknown relatives
and stay just one night
at a tourist cabin
on Red Willow Lake
when all you wanted
was to be like other kids
and play in the water
like an 8-year-old girl
but he told you beware
there are always snakes
in the water and dead
bodies beneath the surface
with drop-offs and quicksand
ready to swallow you up
so you must stay fully dressed
because monsters always look
for little girls in bathing suits.

AS IF YOU WERE
to Carl Christensen, 1942-1983

You reached out to me
after all these years
through an old friend.

I've been in touch with Ralph.
He dedicated his book to your memory.
I recall you telling me what a boon
he was in your early days
in the emptiness of East Texas.

Years before we floated
high in the Berkeley air!
Kingfishers flapping our crazy wings,
diving for a PhD. We missed our prey.
We plunged to earth, academic misfits,
aground in Illinois and New Mexico.

Once at the farm in Berwick
you walked into the August fields,
wrote down the reasons, and called it
What I Learned from the Corn.
It made me laugh and forget
California for a moment.

In New Mexico you showed me how and why
we should camp in the Sandia Mountains
in a driving rainstorm. It washed away
all of our lingering scholastic regret.

I still read your poems, savor your drawings,
hold your animation magic in my mind's eye.
Do you know I saved your letters?
I would like to answer each one again,
tell you everything, and coax
another magical reply from you.

AS THEY SAY

You were deemed a troublemaker
as far back as I remember. Of course
you had an overabundance of freckles.
Mostly I recall your vivid orange-red hair.
As little kids we crawled behind the sofa.
You stuck a bobby pin in the outlet.
It sent sparks igniting the mohair.
In the smoldering of my mother's alarm,
you became, as they say, a bad influence.
That was the last time we played together.
And why spark up that memory now?
How old were we, 3 or 4? By now
you're probably somewhere in prison,
or a grave, but who knows? You might
be a big shot at the power company.

BALTIMORE

There had been passion and charm
in our 3rd floor walk-up. Always we had
blooming flowers and fresh ideas in spring.
But by winter the war was expanding,
squatting with us in the attic apartment.
We couldn't see around it. I remember
how you stared out the oval window
overlooking Charles Street.
You said our presence in Vietnam
was making sense to you.
I had an induction notice
and friends who left for Canada.
It was the only time we argued.
Then the unplanned pregnancy,
as if we stumbled into Cambodia,
the trip wires and pits with spikes,
the snipers and threats.
Driving back from D.C. after the act,
the night ravaged us, your hemorrhaging
and our fear at the ER. Already blackmailed
for more cash by the sotted doctor
who smoked during the procedure.
We tried to clean the car seat.
Nothing worked. We were too young
for Baltimore and the bloody war.

BELOVED

You were always the one who shouldered sadness,
who could tell me how to comfort our daughter.

In your hospital room the calendar is ready
to circle another day, to cycle another shift.

You'll just lie there for days and break another record.
You'll be tomorrow's gossip in the nurses' station.
You cannot speak but you challenge every prognosis
and even the inevitable morphine.

Loved ones are jailed with you in this comfort-care lockup,
when they wanted you home to die in your own bed
with your beloved cats.

The palliative nurse tells us
those who live quietly die quietly.
Everything is channeled, monitored.
The room is dark and silent.
There is no reason for another day.
Now you can go,
go to all the places you didn't get to.
Beloved, let go and go.

You wanted no ceremony,
no memorial, no eulogy.
Famously you said,
Let's not get too sentimental!
En route to the ER you protested,
Don't tell me things are going to get better!

Clocks tick away like a time bomb.
You were young and unstoppable.
Between each click is everything.

Clocks tick away like a time bomb.
Now, as you die and leave us,
between each click is emptiness.

BODY & SOUL

I still see myself
as the person I was.
Vibrant old affairs
become camouflaged
in the faded pages
of dusty calendars.
I'm not the same.
But I'm the same.
Everything changes.
Nothing changes.
I know it's me.
I know it's not.

CABINETMAKING

I would be a worker in wood
and create a fine cabinet to hold
the things you cherish in this world.
It would have a secret compartment
designed to hide your troubles.
I will combine cherry and walnut
with accents of birdseye maple.
The cherry wood comes from
the American black cherry fruit tree.
All I can say is it is exquisite because
in places it is almost a light pink color,
then it ranges all the way to reddish-brown.
I will drive to a dealer in North Carolina
to select flawless eastern black walnut.
Its tight-grain in the sapwood can look
almost creamy white but in the heartwood
it turns to a dark chocolate color with
a purple tint. Imagine the amber glow
of embellishments in birdseye maple.
Did you know they compare the eyes
grown in the maple to saltwater pearls?
There will be no flaws in my cabinet.
I will sand with the finest grit for days.
I will apply ten coats of tung oil
and it will reach perfection for you
before my hand-waxed final touch,
but alas, I am hounded by my restlessness.
I bounce and ricochet from one thing
to another. From this to that, I bob
unproductively. I have no patience.

I confess I am no cabinet maker.
I am profoundly in love with you.
I apologize for misrepresenting this.
If I could, I'd create a cabinet to hold
the things you cherish in this world.
It would have a secret compartment
designed to hide your troubles.

CANTALOUPE

When I see cantaloupe
I also see the helplessness
of a 12-year-old girl
headed for kidney failure
because you explained how
just the smell of cantaloupe
(previously sumptuous to me)
was nauseating to you because
your family drove a Ford pickup truck
and had no normal car like everyone else
which was embarrassing enough
to be dropped off at school
but in the summer to earn extra cash
your father raised cantaloupe
and he would park the pickup
by the crossroads and sell them
on Saturday but on this special Saturday
your mother (who eventually had 8 kids)
was about to give birth to her 6th
and the family piled into the truck
to head into town to the hospital
but the cab was already crowded
with too many brothers and sisters
and you were the oldest girl and told
to ride in the back with the melons
but you were sick that day with what
would later be diagnosed as a deep
infection in your femur and you
had a raging fever and realized
there was hardly any room at home
for another sister and your leg throbbed
and your temperature spiked
and melons rolled and you were told

to wait there in the hospital parking lot
and guard the melons because you
were no longer young and you sat alone
and your nostrils tightened as you gagged
and felt disease surround you
and forever lodge itself there
in the sweet smell of cantaloupe.

CIGAR ROLLERS

They were tagged as intellectuals,
owing to their tradition
of lectors reading aloud
as the rollers rolled
coronas, panetelas, torpedoes.
This was a college without name,
but it taught the liberal arts.
Listening to all those books,
even newspapers being read aloud,
like a wrapper leaf holding them together.
Then machines arrived to replace them.
They had listened to their history books.
They understood progress.
They made a toast to the future,
greeting the last paycheck with a wink,
as if to say, go ahead, you try
pleasing the aficionado
with your shoddy third-rate cigar.

CLEAR AIR

I am fortunate
to have my love.

She clarifies
my wacky conclusions.

I find my way
to peace with her.

She tells me this plus that
is only my morning fog.

She brings her warmth
that burns off my worries.

I watch them dissipate into
the clear air of her comfort.

COLORADO
to Jack

When you were
surely on your feet,
handsome and footloose,
I didn't know you then,
but I imagine women
glanced your way, perhaps
admiring muscles in your calves,
that summer you worked
in Aspen,

before Vietnam,
before returning to the family farm,
before celebrating your homecoming,
before the bad luck of one leap,
before plunging into dark water,
before immobility,
before architecture.

For decades now
I have watched you
with only your arms
to climb obstacles.
You never complain.

I have wanted to tell you
how much I admire your endurance.
I don't mean to embarrass you
by comparing it
to a mountain range
in Colorado, but
it is equally commanding.

COMRADE

Old fires of our friendship
still flicker. My god,
it's been 30 years since we
conspired to conquer the world.
And now you tell me
you tried to kill yourself.
I listen and try to understand
what cannot be understood.
When the ambulance hauled
your shit-faced ass to the ER,
I imagine you laughing.

In your alcoholic daze
you watched a drunk buddy
lose a thumb when he spaced out
and forgot to throw a cherry bomb.
He held on and bang! Indeed,
a bloody mess to clean up,
but you always managed to joke
about that 4th of July happy ending,
when Jesus Christ entered the ER
and both of you in tandem
discovered your new savior.

During sober days and nights
you clutched the Bible
and whispered your new line,
"Praise the lord. Pass the laughs."
You always looked for a punch line.

After attempting suicide
with a massive pile of pills,
leaving the ICU, I hear you
laughing, loving the irony
and proudly declaring,
"I failed again!"

No one knows what to do
with a suicide survivor.
Your after-care was a big zero
followed by a wasteland
of platitude therapy.
And so, comrade, do I sense
Jesus has left the building and left
you with a drinking problem?
It won't help when they send you
home with a bottle of pills, but I hope
you can spin this tale into more laughter,
perhaps your own comedy special
with a title everyone can relate to—
"I Failed Again!"

CUB SCOUTS

There were 6 or 8 of us
from the neighborhood.
I don't suppose I had a choice.
You took the oath to *Do Your Best!*
I wore an official yellow neckerchief
around my neck over my regulation
dark blue shirt with metal buttons.
We met at Billy's because his mom
was our den mother. Once she made
popcorn balls and we pretended
to be Indians weaving bracelets
with red, white & blue plastic strands.
Our pack symbol was a bear.
We met in a knotty pine basement
with the banner, *Be Prepared!*
For all those now forgotten
important accomplishments,
I do remember my own mother
sewing the badges on my shirt.

DEATH OF A LOVED ONE

We cross Donner Pass in clear sunshine,
then a text from a friend is wrenching.
We cross into Nevada and the landscape
announces an empty power all its own.
We are small. The landscape is boundless.
There were bison here once.
Now a car named after a wild horse
speeds past us into the vastness.
We stop for gas in a small town
where a parade has ended.
The floats with victory banners
of football and homecoming royalty
sit parked, still and abandoned.
Your voice has left the earth.

DESCRIPTION OF A PHOTO DATED JUNE 1968

Received from a friend
who took it and captured
a desolate soul, smitten
with the love of a woman
or more accurately the lack of it.
She didn't join him
driving the 1999.5 miles
from North Beach to Illinois.
But she was present then and there,
still pulsing in his defeated heart,
the summer of '68.

The Kodachrome is faded,
the picture is clear. His face
of loss, blank looking,
standing in waist-high weeds,
holding a puppy with floppy ears.
Behind them, a dilapidated barn
is half collapsed, drooping
like the dog's ears.

Drooping is the theme alright.
You cannot see the disquiet,
the entanglements, the weight
of breakup in his head,
but note the telltale
clutching of the puppy
to his dismal heart.

DISCHARGE OF A BASIC AIRMAN

Barely into boot camp
maybe it was flying on acid
and reporting a buddha smiling
in his night-vision binoculars.
His punishment was to mow the grass
with a push mower—this was not a penalty,
but a welcomed march to the promised land,
the opportunity to message what would be
visible from the Major's office window.
The letters mowed in the grass:
AIR FARCE SUCKS
beside a giant peace sign.

DISTANCE

In the flat prairie of Illinois
you can get your arms around
the 80 acres your grandfather farmed.
It's right there, fenced off, easy
to distinguish, even walkable.
But in Nevada, Arizona, New Mexico,
mountains and desert are overwhelming.
Vast waterless land is beige and grey,
the color of sand goes on and on.
Faraway mountains are dark blue,
but sometimes they turn purple.
Someone might call it indigo.
Behind the mountains, white clouds
ascend to a lighter blue sky.
Someone might call it azure. Higher still
wisps of thin clouds float gauzelike
in the azure. Nothing here relates
to being raised on the Rock River
where the downtown, the school,
the football field, the A&P grocery,
the park, the swimming pool, the library,
the fire station, the Oldsmobile dealer—
they were all 3 blocks apart. Here in this
breathtaking landscape images of myself
appear in the distance, small like Dixon.

DRIVING THROUGH YELLOWSTONE

I watched a bear disappear
and couldn't say if it
was male or female,
but by recent estimates
it was one of 728 in the park.

I am not inclined to photograph my food
to send pictures of what's on my plate,
and I'm not judging those who do.
Generations have their own ways.
I've spent more years without
a camera in my phone whereas
some have never been without one.
I just watched.

It wasn't a black bear.
so it had to be a grizzly,
perhaps 400 to 500 pounds,
but that's just my guess.
A photo might have helped
to estimate, but it doesn't matter.
Imagine how difficult it must be
to actually weigh a bear.

This bear crossed the road
and vanished straight
into the lodgepole pines.

That's all. It was one bear
crossing a road. It wasn't scary
like a bison outrunning you.

They say the bison here
pose more danger than bears.
Still, I didn't get out of the car.

There was no risk, just the delight
of sighting the dark brown eyes.
The tan head was led by a strong snout.
Stocky front legs clawed the ground.
Silver-blond shoulder muscles flexed
and swayed. Big rump fur shimmied
under the bright orange of a morning sun.
It strolled then bolted off fast as a horse.
I'm sorry if you'd prefer a photo,
but here's an unshot bear.

EDWARD AND ME

This unavailing search for what?
Is there a lesson back home
from things long fallen away,
like a small town's newspaper?

I watched tears well in the eyes
of a middle-aged man, a typesetter
setting his last hot metal edition
of the *Evening Telegraph*, as he
racked a headline backwards
that would read, *Final Edition*.

After the newspaper closed,
he racked milk at the Borden Dairy
with its oversize mascot at the gate,
where the gallon milk jugs were glass
with wire handles and rolled wood spindles,
four jugs per metal rack, stacked eight high.
Elsie was a friendly cow,
but the work inside was a cold job.

I remember how his name was stitched
in red letters on a white oval on his coat.
He was no Ed or Eddie. He was Edward.

I was just a kid who lost a paper route.
Still, being canned together
when the newspaper went kaput,
it meant we shared something,
Edward and me, back then.

ELEVEN DISPLACED STANZAS

1
this abides in the stillness of a lover's lane dillydally in the dark,
this is the brief pause in an opera where the lights dim and she
is a diva preparing to hit the high note in a moment's breath

2
when you added an exclamation point
to your signature, I didn't know what
you were thinking, but it does impress

3
it was a long time ago and when you asked,
"by the way, are you into any mescaline?"
please forgive me if I dropped the ball

4
exuberance in this enraptured faith
befalls the novices, caught in their alluring fervor
like a spontaneous embrace, seductive and clutching

5
fleeing the city, the flight from siren and strobe
we arrive at the upstate lake where we hear only
the sound of trolling boats sputtering home at dusk

6
it needed no persuasion, the midnight stillness,
thickets of delicate hair, exposed and readied,
preparing for the joyful feel of exploration

7
relax now and float in the sultry corpus of this bond
as it winds a steady bandage for our wobbling
in the dizzy flow that grasps and holds our aging hands

8
did you think about purchasing the ab exercise device
when you learned it could fold up to fit under the bed
or how easily it could be stashed in a closet, even the attic

9
local businesses define relationships to the old bastard
at his bustling visitation, their overflowing floral arrangements
competing in deepest sympathy, signed with a company name

10
Harold embraced misbegotten totems of the sugar empire
stacked up one upon one with impregnable ease
until his life collapsed, gulp, gulp, gulp

11
before this courtroom of plump for picking
you are summoned to appear and be humble
and brave as you are sentenced to stop eating

FISHING IN CANADA

When I was sixteen
I didn't understand
my father's desire
to drive all the way
to International Falls, MN,
where he hired a bush pilot
with a pontoon plane
to fly north to a fish camp
and land on a lake
unreachable by car,
somewhere in that unknown
godforsaken Ontario woods.

I assumed it would be
a torturous week away.
There wouldn't be radio,
television or a telephone.
How insane! Actually, punishing!
I was going steady with my first
True Love and you know that feeling.
Who would want to head
for the north woods with him
when I could have been with her?

If it was a Howard Johnson's Motel
or a Holiday Inn with a pool,
there would have been a phone
and I could have called her.
But this would be lonely,
a phoneless place with no way out.
The pilot would drop us off
and not return for a week.

We landed on the water.
Ashore, we were greeted
by my dad's two close friends.
There was Doc (who was a dentist)
and Algot (fellow immigrant from Sweden).
The 4 of us stayed in a one-room cabin.
There was an outhouse, no running water,
no electricity. The first night we played poker
with the light from oil lamps. I dreaded
listening to 50-year-old codgers, these fools
who paid to be stranded for a week.
But they offered me a beer.
I didn't get that at home.
It made a good impression.
I learned a lot about poker.

Then up at dawn and outside,
where they showed me how
to make a campfire safe,
to boil lake water with one pot,
to cook on the rocks with a skillet.
I warmed to the morning ritual,
bacon, eggs, coffee by the fire.

The first day on the water
a guide led the way.
Dad and me in one boat,
Doc and Algot in another.
We were told to keep in eyesight
but at times almost disappeared,
nearly losing them in the vastness
of intertwined lakes and islands.

Nothing but trees and sky,
and water so clean
I could see to the bottom.

My dad knew about fishing. I didn't.
He taught me how to target
Walleye and Northern Pike.
My reel would charge and bingo—
it was me who was hooked.
The pike are always challenging
and I couldn't resist the challenge.

There was a shore lunch ritual.
I learned how to filet a fish.
Fried Walleye was delicious.
I looked forward to the nights
with poker, beer, and old codgers.

As a teenager I didn't appreciate
my father. It took years to realize
what he accomplished
fishing in Canada.

FOOTBALL COACH

To his tribute,
I cannot remember
if we won or lost.
There was one time
during football practice
he praised my effort.
I tackled the shit
out of a sled dummy
with my head. Concussion
was not a word in high school.
He was a decent teacher
who taught Algebra
and Drivers' Training.
I imagine he picked up
extra bucks coaching.
To his tribute,
I made it through Algebra.
He wore thick glasses,
the kind we called
Coke bottles. He rode
a bicycle to school
when all the teachers
drove cars. He wasn't
a typical coach.
To his tribute,
I cannot remember
if we won or lost.

FOR AN ANONYMOUS ANCIENT FRIEND
(possibly named Owen)

Do you remember another century?
Two Young Turks at dusk surreptitiously
drove down a country road with fear
of being busted, the adrenaline rush,
dashing into a cornfield with machetes
to appropriate a truckload of chagrin.
Absolutely no one got high as a kite
on that pilfered harvest of ditch weed.

Over a dozen US Presidents preside
over the tenure of our friendship.
Your presidential impersonations equal
the best of SNL. Your standup kills when
you hike up your pants, mess up your hair
and spout an exposé of Capitol hypocrisy.
It leaves us rolling in the aisles when you
appoint yourself Governor of a red state
and then a blue. When you become
another clown we elected,
we are left helplessly howling.
When you re-enact City Council snafus,
our stomachs ache from laughter.
We are indebted to your mastery of history,
your beloved Cardinal baseball theories,
your anecdotes from childhood to now
and your welcoming childlike glee
when we get together. It's showtime!

If friendship includes forgiveness—
when the beginning of your sentence
interrupts the middle of ours—
how could we not forgive you?
You are the Dean of Unbridled Eruption,
Manchild of Communal Hilarity,
Special Master of Merrymaking.
We forgive you for making us
cry from laughing. We remain
grateful and now we're all high as a kite
on the inexhaustible harvest of laughs.
Ancient friend, encore,
encore, encore!

HAIKU AFTER ELEVEN WEEKS OF KETO

empowerment grows
waistband two inch smaller now
buy new underwear

HERE

The two of us in the pandemic
learned to relish the comfort
of stay-at-home. Yet now
as covid variants decline
and masks are removed,
we remain inclined
to snuggle in our bungalow
while the world restocks
new endangerments.
And we cannot escape Ukraine.

We have a home, food,
family and friends. Here
there are no bombs exploding.
Our life is not interrupted.
We have our touchstones
and take comfort in our daily rituals.
I will make our morning coffee
while you will make our bed.
You will read the paper in your chair.
I will read the news online in mine.
Yet we cannot escape Ukraine.

We will compare thoughts,
joke over our breakfast so late
it extends into afternoon.
The day leans in, in harmony
you and your crosswords.
me and my poems.
Yet we cannot escape Ukraine.

Often while preparing dinner
we include a momentary dance.

Then, bring on the *Newshour*,
watch the *Warriors* win we hope,
pursue laughter and let the night
ease into mutual backrubs.
Yet we cannot escape Ukraine.

We become boundless
and for another night
let the unforeseen
remains unseen.
We are content and share love.
We cannot ask for more.
Yet we cannot escape Ukraine.
Not even here.

HEY YOU

Your graceful beauty
and your gentle voice,
you clutched me
that first time I saw you.
It put me in bird panic
with overcharged feathers.
I might just as well
have crashed
headfirst into plate glass.
Nervous, and in awe.
I was speechless.
But you, you persist
for all this time, until
the cows come home,
until hell freezes over.
I mean for good, for keeps.
Hey you, you're my one
and only love at first sight.

HIGH SCHOOL HOMECOMING DANCE

Gold paint on cardboard cutouts
highlighted by blue spotlights—it
transformed the school gym
into a rococo night of courtship,
named and promoted on posters as
An Evening at the Palace of Royals.
(The boys football team were the *Dukes*
and the girls were *Duchesses*.)
There under the basketball hoop
amidst 18th century gilded cardboard chairs
with castle walls from the 14th century
(stapled to the bleacher seats),
the young duke set foot in the fantasy,
his hand touching the silky bare back
of his duchess in her sleeveless formal
on this night resplendent in faux moonlight.
You can see him exploring, clutching
for curves and falling in love
like quicksand. One minute
the hair of his duchess sways to a sparkling waltz.
Under magnificent chandeliers of paper mache,
their dance is a perfect box pattern.
Then, the unforeseen williwaw,
the cut-in by another duke and she's gone.
Imagine him looking down at the floor,
suddenly realizing he's alone at the free throw line,
standing there in cummerbund and rented tux,
another forlorn male member of the nobility.

HOSPITAL BED

After many fraught hospitalizations,
you always rallied to come home

and climb the stairs in victory.
But this is different, it's the first time

you have come home to this,
a hospital bed in the living room.

You won't climb the stairs again,
but we don't talk about it.

This will not be acknowledged
and I don't know what to say.

We are cheering for you to rally.
Show us you want to do it again.

We are the helpless ones too.
Show us you want to do it.

We are the helpless ones.
Show us you want to.

We are helpless.
Show us.

HOW TO WRITE A LOVE POEM

Consider your life an accumulation of forgotten facts
and recall the missed opportunities. Place it all in boxes,
including memorabilia, photos and newspaper clippings.
Have a plan to sort it out before you die, but in the meantime,
think about things that are obvious, *prima facie,* clearly numbered.
Make some rules, for example:

#1
Royal blue, not a good color for a big house,
especially a Victorian house,
unless it's on the eastern shore,
facing the Atlantic, say in New Jersey
or somewhere in Greece.
Even there, the choice of royal blue fails frequently.

#2
Shouts made in anger without thinking are not retractable unless
they're at a political rally and on the right side of history.

#3
The Catholic Church will be abandoned as a sinking boat
as the last faithful parishioners bail water in reverse,
filling it from the sea.

#4
The muse's whisper might unfold words in sand,
you might listen and hear a whale's romance,
feel the electricity in the ocean undercurrents,
see the horizon drifting in and out of clouds,
this is when you will draw letters in wet sand,
I love you, and add your initials for clarity.

I KNOW, I KNOW

I feel like a child who has fallen
from his bike in his own driveway—
scraped a knee on gravel, skinned an elbow
or cut his hand a bit—squealing with big tears.

I begin to sway when nothing makes sense
and you steady me. I can feel it happen
when you walk into the room. Your calming
grace. You bandage my embarrassments.

I hear you say it's okay and then it is.
I can fix things around the house,
but you fix the things I can't heal
when I hear you say *I know, I know.*

I MUST TELL YOU ABOUT MY DREAM

Of course, it was disconcerting,
insinuating instantaneous death.
We were holding hands in an airplane.
when the plane exploded! Imagine
to die that way, to be blown into
smithereens in the stratosphere.
And to make matters worse,
we hadn't finished our G&Ts.
Yet, on the bright side, it did resolve
one of us being left alone to mourn.

IMPRESSIONS FROM LYDIA KRÜGER'S DOSSIER
to Carol

You have set out the pathways like a priestess.
As if we were sitting down to dinner in the sea,
truth finds its way in the saltwater, not in sand
nor the soil of fungi. You arrange the currents,
sleeping with seahorses, entanglements in seaweed,
connections glow like a reef with bright edicts:
When your stomach is empty, you will not be hungry.
Monkeys are never in charge in the water.
Life is not lived in high heels.
Kneel but do not pray or remove your shoes.
If it resembles fishing, it is not a sport.
This is why some parents never wanted children.
The harmony of self is an empty mirror facing you.
This is my interpretation, as if it made sense to say,
I do not wait for the dentist when I have no teeth.
My head and tail respond in unison to your wishes.
I like to stay in one place no matter how risky,
seek nourishment at all times, mate for life
and hide. It is not the Garden of Eden,
although some will think it is. If my camouflage
is unrecognizable to you, don't ask to kiss me,
just come forward and dance. If you follow me
I'll change directions and wait for you. Pretend
that I am a clown who can balance on your thigh.
I could go on and on. There are endless questions.
For example, considering one particular folio,
are you saying no horse swims well with a saddle?
Or do I detect something critical about legs?

IMPROBABILITY

we have
separate names

but together
there is a rope
held between us
unwavering

it is unfathomable
for us to let go

it is likelier
to see golden whales
washed up in the Sahara

with the color of sand
and the sand's shifting
adding to the improbability

JOHNNY McGUIRE

I remember my grandfather
protectively holding me in his arms
or taking my hand to walk downtown.

I recall his bedtime story about a horse
pulling a sleigh from the farm into town
to take my mother to school when snow
closed the road to their tin lizzie.
I asked him to tell it again and again.
I delighted in his back rubs.

At the barbershop I sat on his lap
for my first haircut. We returned on schedule
and with his coaching I found the confidence
to sit alone on an elevated seat atop the big chair.
I became a boy king. After each haircut
we found our way to Kresge's 5 and 10
to garner a new toy for my accomplishment.

He died when I was in second grade.
I was too small to be a pallbearer or understand death.
Touching his embalmed head in a casket, it didn't feel right.
It was too hard. That stays with me. But going to the cemetery
was like going to the park. He would have enjoyed seeing me
running around, playing hide-and-seek behind tombstones.

JOHNNY UNDERHILL

He lived across the street where the slope of the land
dropped precipitously down. There were no curbs.
We lived uphill in the aspiring grass of a lush green yard.
Johnny's yard was dry dust or mud after rainfall.
It was like his surname plunged him there. Underhill.
..
When I was a kid, Johnny was big to me, but he was short.
My parents said he stunted his growth with cigarettes.
He smoked Lucky Strikes and rolled the pack proudly
in his t-shirt sleeve. He snapped a Zippo lighter emblazoned
with a pin-up girl. He cussed. He had a homemade tattoo
on his hand, self-inflicted. He'd stick and poke with a needle
and India ink. We got to watch. He didn't flinch or shed a tear.

If there's a Napoleon Complex, Johnny had it in spades.
Only 4'-10" as a high school junior. I stood in awe of him in 4th grade.
Right to his mother's face he'd shout, "Hey, woman! Get me breakfast!"
I tried that at home with very poor results.

Once a rat jumped in their empty oven and he fired
a shotgun blast into the stove. Blew up the kitchen.
I imagine I admired his aggression. I had never seen a rat
so dead. Johnny always left a big impression.

Once, after a huge snowfall he rolled down all the windows
of his neighbor's new Chevrolet and shoveled the car full of snow,
front and back, all the way up to the top of the seats.
The police came. He denied it. Everyone knew it was Johnny.

My trouble broke out when my dad bought a new Oldsmobile,
a Ninety-eight with a rocket and stars on the steering wheel horn.
I rushed across the street to tell Johnny. He asked me what color it was.

When I said grey, he punched me and sneered, "I don't like grey."
I ran home with a bloody nose. So ended Johnny for me.

Everything went downhill for Johnny. He called in a false alarm
just to take a shot at the firetruck with his pellet gun.
Next, he shot at a neighbor's cat. Soon he was in juvenile detention.
By the time I entered high school, he had stolen a car and followed up
with a robbery that led to his first stint in the big house in Joliet.
After 4th grade, I never spoke to him again. There were actors
like James Cagney and Edward G. Robinson, but they were just acting.
For the real deal, I visualize Johnny Underhill, dead or alive.

JOURNEY OF HUMANITY

A smoking engine framed
our forage for humanity.
The old-school mechanic
delivered the conundrum:
Where's the dip stick?

Approaching from the east,
approaching from the west,
we are fellow travelers
united in the mile-high city
to journey into cherished times
as the dearest of friends.
We parachute amid edibles,
walk amid western art.
No one else will juxtapose
William F. Cody and Buffalo Bill
with hobos versus bums.
When there's trouble, ask:
Where's the dip stick?

No one but you and yours, me and mine,
will stroll the downtown sculptures
in Sioux Falls in search of the falls,
or wend our way to celebrate
special processed American meat,
or feast alone in the Kahler Grand Café,
or drive the driftless area to Taliesin,
or discover the joys of Milwaukee,
the hotel inside the department store,
the inadmissible parking garage,
the sailor's knock on the door,

the architect's mind in the museum,
the pathway to the Pabst Theater,
the guitar in the hands of John Hiatt,
the voice of Lyle Lovett, the Burg,
the chicken fried steak, the G&Ts,
the artist's fateful vape and slow sink
to the floor, while we, still standing, ask:
Where's the dip stick?

JUST LIKE THAT

The night my father died
his hospice nurse predicted it.
She knew the signs, the way
he refused to go to bed. As he
insisted on sitting up in a chair
with his open eyes, he might
have been on the lookout
for the angel of death
when his heart collapsed
just like that.

Normally I am a hearty sleeper.
But this morning, still dark out,
I couldn't get back to sleep.
It's not like me. I recall the nurse
saying not being able to sleep
is common when you're about to die.
Is this insomnia or the Grim Reaper?
Aw, shit, not today, not me,
not now, no way. I've got laundry
to do and tomorrow there's trash
to haul to the curb. Forget it, not
happening, not on a Monday, not
just like that.

LEAVING A MOTOR COURT IN UTAH

I pushed on until we pulled over
approaching the Great Salt Lake.
It was another day on the road
without, as they say, going all the way.
We were young and confounded
and we weren't Mormons. You said
you didn't know if you could handle it.
Of course, we needed sleep and there
was only one bed in the small room.
Then that morning's indelible radiance
floated for miles over the salt flats
when we left a Motor Court in Utah
pretending to be a married couple.

LOOSE THREADS AND POCKETS WITH HOLES

The museum displays ancient clothing,
patterns sewn with intricate mistakes,
delicate silks with intentional wine stains,
wool and jute with lace for amusement,
loose threads and pockets with holes.

Memory is my enemy and my friend.
What you taught me was false.
Perhaps you didn't know any better.
What they taught you was false too,
loose threads and pockets with holes.

MAYBE IT WAS JUST A DREAM

There is silver mercury in their veins.
They appear to be thieves without teeth,
loading boats hidden in the backwater
by a river named Pumping Heart.
The men move at night and stretch
hides of wild animals over hollow logs.
It could be zebra skin or a striped gazelle.
Blonde women wear long green gowns
made of woven banana leaves.
They pound music from the drums.
Wood-boring beetles eat their way through,
leaving sawdust inside the drums.

Everything made sense inside the dream.
Awake it is quagmire, though once
in the 70s, I did sell African drums
in a headshop in western Illinois.
They were like the ones in the dream,
purchased from a man from India,
who had a company called African Imports.
A loyal customer with blonde hair once
returned a drum with wood-boring beetles,
but she wasn't wearing banana leaves,
unfortunately.

MY GARDEN

I find myself comfortable here
in this place where once I languished
among my annual wilted failures.
I enjoy sitting on my bench
in the low sun of late afternoon
admiring the variety, counting the colors,
trying to recall the names of umpteen flowers.
It is thriving now, but this was built on nothing
but dead loss in my rookie years. Most assuredly,
I didn't know what the hell to do. I over-watered.
Plants died. I under-watered. Plants died. I fumbled.
Flop after flop. Eventually I learned to take my time
and plan. Some amended soil here, added mulch there,
fertilizer every other Saturday and voila! Marigolds
took flight. The sight of the hibiscus generated hope.
One red geranium called for a blue delphinium.
I looked for the simple solutions. Snapdragons
behind the petunias just made sense. Daisies belonged
in front of the irises. Some things came freely.
A volunteer hollyhock was delivered by a bird
or perhaps a squirrel. The challenge of a rose remains,
but I resist it. Remarkably, there are no weeds
in my garden, at least none that I see.

MY MOTHER SURVIVED THE 1918 PANDEMIC

I hadn't thought about it
until Covid-19 arrived.
She died years ago
and never spoke of 1918.
I have her picture at age ten
in a wagon pulled by a goat.
My grandfather made it
as a gift for her and painted
a daisy on the side. All this was
written on the photo's backside,
including the goat's name,
Arcella, and the year, 1920,
but not a word about surviving
the Spanish Flu. Who knows?
She was born on an 80-acre farm
a dozen miles from town
She lived to be over 100
and never mentioned it once.

NEW YEAR'S EVE 1949

I stepped over any breach with them.
Their views had shortcomings,
but they were always loving.
They struggled with parenting
just as their parents did. But they
made sure I would struggle less.
I can hear the old Philco radio,
big band music unconfined
as my parents float past me
sliding over kitchen linoleum
dancing to Guy Lombardo
and the Royal Canadians
and I am a child witnessing
the arrival of the Fifties
with a spinning tin noisemaker
and a flaming sparkler, and
that feeling that everything
is just about to blossom,
counting down to midnight,
auld lang syne lyrics
embedded in afterglow.

NOTHING HELPS
to Denis Baylor, 1940-2022

Helplessness stunned me once
in an earthquake. Without warning
the house rolled, windows shattered,
pictures on the wall took flight,
photos of family and friends crashed
face down in broken glass.

Now, the news of your death stuns us.
How can we not visualize you down
in the midst of your beloved game?
Was it on the green, the tee or fairway?
It doesn't matter. Perhaps your heart quit
before you reached the ground, but
the time before the ambulance arrived
is unimaginable. We are unprepared.
We say you were too young
because you left too soon.

Rationalizations attempt to comfort us—
you died doing what you loved,
you didn't linger from a stroke,
you didn't end up in a nursing home—
we hear our voices,
but nothing helps.

NOW

My love vanished
for half a lifetime.

We were reunited
due to a photograph.

Marvelous happenstance,
destiny, wild good luck.

Seeing the Pacific Ocean
was utter fulfillment.

Now her love for me
is more than the ocean.

OLD FOLKS HOME

It was on the next corner,
just down from our house,
a 3-story Queen Anne
with a wrap-around porch
lined with rocking chairs.

We rode our Schwinns there
to gawk at the motion of ancient ones,
their gray and white hair, the shawls
and their bygone bodies rocking
like skeletons. We pictured nothing
but bone dust, us neighborhood kids.
We delighted in racing across their yard
to hear the shouts, *Scram! Get off the grass!*
We were marauders!
And then we'd pedal fast to flee
the imagined pursuits by old timers
who never left the porch.

Now as an old codger I realize
it was probably as much fun for them
to marvel at the energy of 10-year-olds
fleeing from the old folks home.

ON BECOMING WALLPAPER

There is joy in my disappearance in plain sight.
My lack of importance giggles me.
Around younger folks
(who now encompass everyone),
I am increasingly irrelevant,
present but unseen, no need to participate,
no wish to keep up, no desire to achieve.
I watch you compete for a role
in your struggling stages of discontent.
I have none of it. I've left it all behind.
I recall as a child at Halloween
being costumed up by my mother
in a white sheet with slits for eyes
to trick-or-treat anonymously.
I triumphed as a ghost, my bag
of goodies overflowing. I relish
the excitement now. I walk
among you. I watch. I hear you.
I gather your tales like a ghost
collecting your goodies,
no need for a sheet.

ONE DAY

It was just a picnic
on a single afternoon.
Why revisit this
wee morsel
of my young days?
57 years have passed.
What difference
does it make that
we left Baltimore
to spend the day
in the salty air,
where we spread out
a blanket on the shore,
joked about acting like
a couple in a French film
with baguette & cheese
and a bottle of wine.
Seagulls watched us
and we watched them.
When a bold one approached,
we named him *Charles de Gull*
and surrendered our scraps.
Nothing is connected now
as we imagined it would be.
Even you died years ago.
Even this mist in the air,
particles floating untethered,
nothing but words,
leftovers, remnants,
a crumb, one day
on Chesapeake Bay.

ONE SUMMER ON THE RIVER IN A BOAT NAMED MY BELLE

Somebody's uncle let us use her
and when the river called us
(that July, almost nightly)
she promised romance
whenever we pushed off
in that mahogany dreamboat
with her Canadian hull—
such a beauty—she could run
in the shallows, turn on a dime,
move away from barge lights,
slip into the back channels
where we could skinny-dip,
then share a towel to dry
and let our hands trust
a little closer each night
to explore secret places
under a purple blanket,
her name in gold thread
embroidered on it, My Belle.

OTHERWISE

Tell me you want me to be a monk
and I will appear in a brown itchy robe,
rough hemp rope for a belt,
my exposed calves and ankles
leading to crude sandals,
the monk beard, of course—all
the look you desire
without rising before dawn
without lauds
without work in the fields
without vespers
without sleeping on a wooden cot
without the abstinence,
especially not the abstinence!
Otherwise, I'm 100% monk
vowing to please you.

PARABLE OF THE SILK HANDKERCHIEF (TO BE READ TO A CHILD AT BEDTIME WITH A SILK HANDKERCHIEF)

Once upon a time,
there was a time without tears.
Far in the future
there was a perfect mom,
her golden bronze skin,
her golden bronze eyes,
her golden bronze hair.
Her golden bronze gown
trailed after her, her children followed
like little golden bronze moons
orbiting a golden bronze planet
in a golden bronze sky
where everything felt as smooth
as this handkerchief. Here,
hold it in your hand.
Take it and you will dream
dreams of golden bronze.

PATAGONIA, AZ
to Bob & Elise

I assume because of age
this is your last habitat
or to put it bluntly, the place
you have chosen to die,
but not today!

We climb with caution.
You have warned us—
the driveway is a dry creek bed.
We adjust to the elevation,
over 4000 feet, and try
to patch up all the years apart.
We were bearded chaps
from another century
and they the pretty coeds
in black & white photos.

After 56 years, we hug each other
and settle into the dizzy joy of reunion
and recollections from our college when
the days were filled with *Veritas* and longing.

I'm enthralled by the view from your porch,
this high desert and the mountain ranges.
It's the feeling I feel at the ocean.
Here the four of us sit and find one another
on this land where we are small and then no more.

The border patrol stop en route from Tucson
gave us pause, but it wasn't meant for us.
You point out the passageway to the east,
the inlet that runs south to Mexico.

Unchanged for centuries, this is the place
passed through on the journey for answers.

One appreciates the color of Red Mountain
when the sun is just so. And here in front of me
is a rusted Road Runner holding a rusty snake.

Were we like those hawks you just described?
With eyes to spot targets, wings balanced in flight,
was that us then in some unclouded blue sky?
We are septuagenarians now and feel the difference,
the wobbling uneven balance of buzzards' wings.
As dusk approaches we observe our bird selves,
a kettle of vultures circling in the distance
heading down for trees and rest for the night.

With the chill of evening, we go inside
to look over photos in our old yearbooks
and the lit mags we edited together.
We could not have imagined then
our visitation tonight with legal weed,
a perfect meal, and good stories.
When you turned on the lights
winding along the wall,
spread through colorful art glass,
over family heirloom crystal,
and you said it had been damaged,
we didn't see any cracks at all,
only the glow from a lifetime ago.
It was a clear night with stars.
Didn't we all sleep soundly
and wake up younger?

PD

Alas, yes, I suffer from it—
Premature Disappointment.

I sense the bad news
coming around the corner.

My friends are dying.
Guess I'll be joining them.

Meanwhile, I'm confined here
in the antechamber of my heart.

Join me here. Ask your doctor
if preemptive discouragement is for you.

PLEASE HOLD

Due to our merger with your bank
we offer solutions to your inquiries.
You received an email this morning
with incomprehensible instructions
on how to access your account.
Thank you for holding your breath.
We appreciate your rage and will ignore it.
We have complicated our merger successfully.
We do our best to make your life more miserable.
Due to our merger your frustration will grow.
We are experiencing increased call volumes
in excess of your life expectancy. Please hold.
We appreciate your irritation as your blood
continues to boil. Please wait for the next
available donkey. Thank you for holding.
To get answers to your questions right now
visit our online Fuck You section. We can assure
that your accounts have transitioned successfully
to another encryption of inaccessible data.
Please hold for the next available zombie.

PORTFOLIO ROMANCE

peace to some
sorrow to others

this one dwindles
that one crashes

others grow miraculously
and romp at the zoo

they promise
a cure for insects

an enchanting hope
uneasy mistrust

the misbegotten dalliance
the unbidden kiss

REACHING YOU

When we separated,
everything about us
seemed buried in a mudslide.
I figured it would take a miracle
to reach you again.

Perhaps there was a pathway
to discover the beauty in the black
oaks dotting the golden hills
of California. I couldn't see it then.

Perhaps there were mountains
with year-round white peaks
in the distance and the ocean—
just impossible for me to visualize.

I locked in on the horizontal
outstretch of corn and beans.
It leveled me and I plowed
into flat western Illinois prairie.

For this to trickle down,
it was inexplicable,
a heaven-sent bubbling up
of a spring in a cornfield, growing
to a stream, to a creek,
to a river, to a confluence,
to a bay, to an ocean
until there was nothing left but
this astonishing phenomenon
of reaching you.

RETURNING TO THE OCEAN AT EL GRANADA

Back then I wanted to escape
from what stunted me.
I was useless as a coloring book
without crayons, even stymied
by the wetsuits bobbing offshore,
black outlines marking time,
waiting for the next colossus
in the lofty surf at El Granada.
Why do that?

Then it was just a place
where rents were cheap,
where I licked my wounds
in a one-room hut,
deep in a eucalyptus grove.
California was vibrant.
A bright blue ocean beside
golden yellow hills. But me,
I languished in my own
chasmic self-pity,
cinder block walls,
grayness, blinds closed.

Today the past is unrecognizable.
The eucalyptus grove is gone.
My wounds have healed.
With you, I am untroubled,
transformed, exuberant,
bright blue and golden.

ROOTS OF MY PRIVILEGE

My mother was well along
in her pregnancy in 1943.
That summer before I was born
riots in Detroit killed 34 people
(25 black / 9 white)
and Roosevelt sent 6000 troops
to enforce a curfew.
I arrived in October,
born in the seventh sign,
a Libra son to a Libra mom,
on her birthday no less.
We lived in a small town
with no black people to know.
The war in Europe ended
just before my second birthday.
Mom stayed home.
Dad managed a shoe store.
My grandparents lived a block away.
Nobody locked any doors.
Everything was reassuring.

SCALING DOWN

Supposedly, or so we try
to proclaim: we don't want
to trouble our children.
Everyone our age whistles
time-to-shrink tunes.
Downsize. Eliminate.
Too many memorabilia,
too many photos,
too many saved letters,
too many books, CDs.
No one will desire
outdated furniture,
china, pots & pans.
Our drawers and shelves
stuffed with cherished folderol.
Can there be richness
saving the bygone?
Useless 8-track tapes,
old AAA maps from car trips,
empty wine bottles to be
cut into tumblers. This
holy mess mixes with the grace
of our romance. We recorded it
in notebooks, and like photos
of our dead parents, how can we
eliminate our own loves?
Meaningless and meaningful
blend into a blurring swill.
We talk about categories:
Keep/Goodwill/Landfill.
Immediately we surrender.
Just the thought of sorting
exhausts us. We shall

embrace the status quo.
We backslide together.
Let our kids decide.
When we are dead
scaling down
will be a breeze.

SEA OF HURRAHS

My dear dead adversary
I did not intend for you
to be engulfed in this sea
like a match tip ignited, you
and your faithful wooden ship
aglow in phosphorus loss.

Now that you are uncuttable
I will put down my blade.
My hand extends in friendship.
No need for subterfuge,
your death and my life
have partnered a truce.

Do you see how it is for us
sailing on the Sea of Hurrahs?
Can you hear the sea shanty?
Hurrah! Sing fare thee well!
Hurrah! Sing fare thee well!
Hurrah! Hurrah! Hurrah!

SEA RANCH

Perhaps if I lived here,
I would accomplish nothing
and be satisfied. To never write
another poem, or even try,
or better, without any need to try.
This thought of being content
surfaces, over and over, watching
whitewater break on the rocks below.
From this outlook, I see the ocean's
magnitude, and my little troubles.
I am tangled in seaweed, bobbing.
I am the descendant of a sea creature
crawling to shore. Why bother?
The grass grows tall in these meadows.
Here, where no lawnmowers are allowed,
the sheep will come to graze. Here
the waves say it, over and over.
I have no words that make sense.

SEPARATE WAYS

I didn't see it coming. No one did.
During that first '65 blackout in NYC,
you and I were fellow grad students.
I thought of us as close friends,
especially after that dark night for hours
walking from Harlem to Times Square,
stopping for a beer in that bar aglow with candles.
It was your helpful idea to assist confused motorists
and direct traffic with flashlights at busy intersections.
The *Times* praised your actions as a Good Samaritan.
You loved art history and would be a thoughtful teacher.
Was it the blackout? Did a painting turn you inside out?
What was it? Within a month, at an otherwise festive party,
you flipped out and slashed a friend with a knife for no reason.
Then you disappeared and abandoned your fellowship.
There was a rumor that you enlisted in the Air Force
with speculation you might be dead. In no time
we all went our separate ways.

SHOES IN THE ATTIC

We didn't think about how hot it was
when we packed away the collection,
your 70s platforms. Prized leather,
ravaged by the summer heat, separates.
Over decades we forgot those shoes,
but how did we lose you?

Everything feels unsettled, a useless pilgrimage
through the day's touchstones—the newspaper
and the mail arrive on time, outside in your garden
the mourning doves show up in pairs, but inside
your cats search and search for you.

I will climb into the attic. I will stand before shoes,
prepared to dust them in adoration, like a shrine.
Sometimes classical FM will play an aria at noon.

SMOKING

I can't stand the thought
of smoking now,
but back in the day,
when we all indulged,
cigarette brands made
an abiding impression.
My god, was anything
more satisfying
than an addiction?
At times it even gave rise
to a sense of victory.
There were associations,
like that first time we tried
as best we could
to love one another
in a bed of uncertainty.
If there was failure
to lament,
it disappeared
in our inhaled glow
when you shared a menthol.
I had never tried one
until that night in Iowa City.
Back then I was hooked
on those Parliaments
with the recessed paper filter.
Over the years it all worked out.
We all quit smoking.
But what a seduction,
that night with a Salem.

SOMETIMES I FEEL LOST

It's like failing to write it down
when importance comes knocking
or a dream you want to recall
vanishes when you wake up.

Only my whiskers thrive.
My thoughts turn vapid.
I'm lost in swampy Florida
with alligators and crocs.

Shit, now I think of Lassie
coming to my rescue
like it's normal to find
Collies in the Everglades.
They say Collies aren't
that smart as dogs go.
Sometimes I feel lost.

STOP EATING HAIKU

my doctor warns me
the fat man in his eighties
will soon disappear

SUBJECT MATTER

There is a tangerine tree in our backyard.
Squirrels have discussions in the branches.

They leap and dance and devour the citrus.
Do you remember what the first time was like
when you were a teenager drunk on sloe gin?

There is a tangerine tree in our backyard.
Squirrels have discussions in the branches.

A pair of fox squirrels proclaim ownership.
This food source will be defended.
They will warn of approaching enemies.

There is a tangerine tree in our backyard.
Squirrels have discussions in the branches.

Occasionally a hawk may threaten from above.
Occasionally a cat may threaten from below.
Occasionally I may appear to be a threat.

There is a tangerine tree in our backyard.
Squirrels have discussions in the branches.

When I approach them, they screech, scold,
squawk and bark. I watch them converse.
This could be subject matter for a poem.

There is a tangerine tree in our backyard.
Squirrels have discussions in the branches.

TAILLIGHTS

I admit something
made me lose control.
My heavy head turned
into a hammer.
I pounded myself silly,
and in turn you too.
I don't know why
I shattered the taillights.
It was my mistake.
It led us nowhere.
It was a Studebaker,
wasn't it?

THE DISAPPEARANCE

You joined the Peace Corp
and disappeared into a tiny village
in Nigeria in the late sixties. We were
friends and when you returned
to the states you brought me
a small carved stool, attributing magical
powers from the Ibibio people.
You said you witnessed a shaman
walk through a solid wall and another
transform into a bird and fly from sight.

You asked to go rabbit hunting on the farm
after a fresh snowfall. You with the only rifle
led us on our walk into the woods where you
made one clean shot. I had never witnessed
such speed as you gutted and cleaned it.
You presented the rabbit skin to me.
Then you took off and I never heard
from you again. It made no sense to me,
but I assumed you knew who you were
and wanted to pass from sight like a mystic.

THE STUDY OF PHILOSOPHY

I know a man who made a rich life in academia.
He was one of the brightest students of his day.
He read the classics and soared to a doctorate.
He published article after article, book after book.
One of the most educated minds imaginable,
I heard him proclaim, "All academics are scum."
I assumed he would know.

I tried to be an academic and failed.
I plunged from an ivory tower
into a pool of hardening work.

I sold shoes and heard my boss say,
"Shoe dogs are scum." I concluded
he meant salesmen like me.

Thus: *Academics + Shoe Salesmen = Scum.*
This is what happens
when you study philosophy.

THINKING OF TRAINS AT THREE IN THE MORNING

Awake. I can't get back to sleep.

No whistles sound tonight. There are no *Now Arriving*
or *All Aboard* announcements. I've missed the train
and I'm stuck at the CB&Q depot back when it
contained a shoeshine stand in the men's lounge,
when businessmen wore wingtips and white shirts with ties,
when the newsstand overflowed with multiple papers,
when the white glazed brick walls of the main waiting room
echoed announcements of 38 arrivals and departures,
every day, people sitting on the huge wooden benches,
the ones with massive armrests to prevent lying down
like tonight as I sit here, isolated with a fool's reminiscence
and these thoughts tend toward vanished trains.

I remember riding on the Zephyr at night from Denver,
the clicking of metal in motion, the gentle sway of the bed.
If only I were on it tonight, I'd be sound asleep.

TOXIC MASCULINITY

It was after the war,
late forties or early fifties,
all the GIs were heroes.
I sat in the yard playing war
with my little GI toys
like tiny dolls for boys.

If I got out of line
my mother warned me to stop
or she'd tell my dad.
It was clear that meant trouble.
He was the boss hog.

My grandmother, mother and sister
wore nothing but dresses and skirts.
My grandfather, dad and I
were the only ones wearing pants.
It probably laid the groundwork.

TUSCARORA TUMBLEWEED

My disappointment in not hearing from you
has festered to disappointment in myself.
Perhaps I should have reached out sooner.
Perhaps I should not have reached out at all.
After all these decades, I don't know
what's left?

There was the time in Tuscarora
where there was nothing but sagebrush
with a potter's wheel that could turn
emptiness into art. You dared to market
a bag of whimsy to NYC's upper crust
and sold the aroma of tumbleweed
to Bloomingdales.

That landscape left us blurred,
wavering in our own failed love affairs.
We were young conscientious objectors
longing for California at a time when
North Beach made sense, briefly
between the beatniks and the hippies.
You told me of the guy who hid in a closet
and paid you to cuckold him, a job
you took more seriously than parking cars.
We sorted mail and fought against the war
until we could not fight and headed home,
prepared to surrender to our failures.
We had so much in common then.

But you know how it goes.
One day at a time turns to the next
and what's left is like wind gusting in Nevada,
blowing tumbleweed over arid land.
You were from Pennsylvania. I from Illinois.
Together, we had never seen anything like it.

VICE PRESIDENT OF FISH

somebody's tired of being so goddamned courteous
when kitchen chairs move to the living room filling with strangers
pretend your daughter is a nun and take the exit path
escape to the jaws of denial
she's caught in the act of yes and body language to boot
and this loser's lucky to stay out of prison
so don't try to get inside his head
put an aquarium in his office for payback
if you think I'm a jokester count my master sergeant stripes
this body may look decrepit but you can't see inside
where the rage of dog tags vibrate like a ticking time bomb
ready to micro-manage the courtship of this horny teenager
in the backseat with your daughter
a decked-out dolly digger who can pop it
a smooth computer geek with an empty reptile wallet
now's the time to hire a hired man and ice it down
forget intellectual property and wrap him in a blanket
sit down and prepare your skin to crawl from the inquisition
under her pregnant skirt begging you please
daddy can my lover boy have a laptop job
can he paint his office chartreuse and sample your cash
until you are ready to spit teeth
did he say he liked a comfortable chair behind a big desk
the nice view with a company car
and keys to the executive washroom
was he just another goofball lounging by the pool
was he as cool as a cucumber in disgrace
roll over and welcome him like he's family
situate him in the office of quality to mind the fish
swimming near him with his title on the door

WE THOUGHT WE KNEW YOU

Before you drove
without stopping
800 miles to us
to tell us of tragedy,
the cancer,
your young wife
dead at 29.
You refused
to spend the night.
You claimed
you would heal
by heading west.
To where?
There were 2 books
in the front seat,
Blue Highways and
Travels with Charley.
You promised to write.
We never heard
another word
from you, of you
and we thought
we knew you.

WHEN I DREAMED OF YOUR PAST

those things you told me about yourself,
the ones you called your indiscretions
became alluring to me as I listened
to your whispers like a priest
aroused by your confession

I heard a curvaceous marble sculpture
draw me toward its curves

your hand cast in bronze
bewitched and beckoned me
with lapis lazuli fingers

finally, you welcomed me inside
your luxurious Bedouin tent
made of black goat hair and sheep's wool,
the ropes were silk, the pallet sumptuous,
the cool temperature inside
welcoming from the desert heat,
until you disappeared

I felt myself fermenting without air
left in a boondoggle of teenage lovesickness

why did I ask?
why did you answer?

WHEN THINGS GOT INTERESTING

One summer in our teens
we spent a brief time on horseback.
Growing up then, you know how
things come and go. Briefly we were
addicted to roller skating,
then bowling and golf. The river
was a big attraction, water skiing
and some fishing. But making out
at the movies always won out over sports.
There were the times when one thing
dominated everything else. Like tennis
or drag racing or playing pool.
But let's face it, kissing a girl
was when things got interesting.

YOU CAN SEE WHERE THIS IS GOING

In an attempt to save the oak grove
by the Cal Bears Memorial Stadium,
protesters chained a piano to a tree
and staged a tree sit-in for 20 months.
They swung from tree to tree like Tarzan,
the soon-to-be vanquished up there
hanging on in their hopeful tethers.

I heard a man at a peace rally
shout with a boomerang voice,
"I don't care what you do
as long as it's militant!"

When the announcer introduces Tiny
and a 400-pound man appears
in a leopard print loincloth,
you're at the carnival sideshow
and you understand the irony.

Once a strong man in Australia
who used to eat razor blades and glass,
but got tired of them,
bet another man $11,000
that he could eat a whole car
within 3 years.

I knew a priest who became bored
listening to confessions.
For penance for their sins
he assigned parishioners to listen
to Barbara Streisand sing "People"
three times in a row.

My doctor is morbidly obese
and a magnificent practitioner
with impeccable bedside manner.

You can see where this is going.
Everywhere there is poetry.

YOU KNOW THE FEELING

You're a passenger without a seat,
your wallet and passport stolen,
abandoned in a foreign land.

Perhaps you're farming parched fields
and more weeds than crops pile up,
like punches in a prizefight.

Jabs of unanticipated misbeliefs,
uppercuts to your pipe dream.
You know the feeling.

Fumbling and desperate,
hankering to hold a winning hand
but it's not poker, it's boxing.

Here's a left hook to your aspiration.
Your mouthpiece is knocked out.
You didn't see it coming.
You know the feeling.
You forgot to duck.

Made in the USA
Middletown, DE
06 January 2023